# She Did It

by Lynn Maslen Kertell
pictures by Sue Hendra

Scholastic Inc.
New York • Toronto • London • Auckland • Sydney • Mexico City • New Delhi • Hong Kong

**Ask for Bob Books at your local bookstore, or visit www.bobbooks.com.**

ISBN 978-0-545-34823-2

12 11 10 9 8 7 6 5 4 3 2 1          11 12 13 14 15/0

Printed in China / 68
This edition printing, January 2011

Dot saw a hill.

Can she go to the top?
Can she do it?

Dot ran. Do it, Dot!

She did it! Dot is at the top.

Dot saw Mat. Can she tag Mat?

Dot fell. Dot did not tag Mat.

Get up, Dot. Do it!

Dot got up. She ran and ran.
Do it, Dot!

She did it! Dot did tag Mat.

# The End